The Wit and Wisdom of Donald J. Trump

by Publius

"Despite the constant negative press covfefe"

— tweet of 5/31/21

Published by [Parker Publishers]

ISBN: [978-0-2206-3602-9]

Printed in [U.S]

TABLE OF CONTENTS

ABOUT THE AUTHOR

Publius is best known for his writing of The Federalist Papers, a series of 85 essays which promoted the ratification of the Constitution of the United States between October 1787 and May 1788, published in various New York state newspapers of the time.

Although he has not published anything new until now, with the sagacity and perspective he has gained as he approaches his three hundredth birthday, Publius has decided that our current political crisis requires careful review and thought about the leading contenders for the presidency in 2024.

Accordingly, Publius has spent more than two years reviewing all the speeches, writings, tweets, press releases, rallies, and utterances of the 45th and 46th U.S. Presidents, including a complete review of classified documents stored in the bathroom at Mar-a-Lago.

From this exhaustive review, Publius has compiled comprehensive lists of the learned and insightful thoughts from these men who are indisputably the two greatest Americans of the current time, and perhaps the greatest since the Founding Fathers.

Now available for the first time to the general public, Publius' two groundbreaking companion books, The Wit and Wisdom of Donald Trump and The Wit and Wisdom of Joseph Biden, should be read by everyone as they consider their vote in 2024.

Preface

Federal Prison Blues (to the tune of "Folsom Prison Blues" by Johnny Cash)

I hear Jack Smith a comin',
He's after me again,
And I gotta get good lawyers,
Or I'm goin' to the pen.
I'm goin' to federal prison,
My lawyers drag it out,
But that Jack Smith keeps on chargin',
I need reasonable doubt.

When I was just a young lad,
The lesson daddy taught,
Is that you can do anything
As long as you're not caught.
But I made an insurrection,
With those right-wing nuts
And I would've been successful
If Pence had any guts.

Rich and poor folks donating
Into my defense fund,
It's me they're still supporting,
Their bank accounts are dunned.
They don't know I am a conman,
That it is all a grift,
But those people keep a-giving,
Don't know they're being stiffed.

Well, if I have to go to prison,
Then I really wouldn't mind,
Cause I'll still have lots of money,
And I'm smarter than Einstein.
I'll run for reelection,
And when the voting's done,
I'll be back inside the White House
Give myself a pardon.

The Wit and Wisdom

The end.